POSTCARDS FROM PLUTO

A TOUR OF THE SOLAR SYSTEM

written and illustrated by LOREEN LEEDY

HOLIDAY HOUSE   NEW YORK

This book is dedicated to those men and women who began the quest to explore our universe, and to those children who will someday continue the journey.

The author wishes to thank Dr. Richard C. Jones for his cosmic advice.

The author also thanks Bruce T. Draine, Professor of Astrophysical Sciences, Princeton University Observatory, for reading this book prior to its publication.

Library of Congress Cataloging-in-Publication Data
Leedy, Loreen.
    Postcards from Pluto : a tour of the solar system / Loreen Leedy.
    —1st ed.
    p.   cm.
    Summary: Dr. Quasar gives a group of children a tour of the solar system, describing each of the planets from Mercury to Pluto.
    ISBN 0-8234-1000-5
    1. Solar system—Juvenile literature.   2. Planets—Juvenile literature.   [1. Solar system.   2. Planets.]   I. Title.
QB501.3.L44   1993   92-32658   CIP   AC
523.2—dc20
    ISBN 0-8234-1237-7 (pbk.)

First we'll fly by the biggest, hottest, brightest object in the solar system— the Sun.

THE SUN

Dear Mom & Dad,
    Did U know that R
Sun is really a ☆?
It is only a medium-
sized ☆, but over 1
million Earths could
fit inside. We can't 🐝
2 close because of the
intense heat (<u>millions</u>
<u>of degrees!</u>)
    Stay cool— Your ☀
              Ray

Mr.+Mrs. Sol Corona
93 Shady Lane
Sun Valley, Idaho
U.S.A.   83353

I am a STAR!

P.S. The Sun has darker, cooler blotches called SUNSPOTS.

SOLAR ECLIPSE

The bowl-shaped holes on a planet or moon are called CRATERS.

Wow! MERCURY is covered with them.

Dear Uncle Freddy,
GUESS THE PLANET—
1) It's closest to the Sun.
2) It has the shortest year (88 Earth days.)
3) It has no water, no air, and no moons.
If you said Mercury, you're right! Also, it is burning hot on the sunny side, and freezing cold on the dark side. Good-bye for now!
Your nephew,
Eric

Freddy Fickle
100 Quicksilver Dr.
Frozenfire, Alaska
99552

I'm hot & cold at the same time!

Sunlight

crater

MERCURY

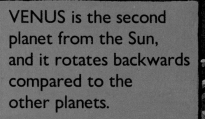

VENUS is the second planet from the Sun, and it rotates backwards compared to the other planets.

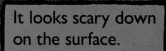

It looks scary down on the surface.

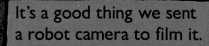

It's a good thing we sent a robot camera to film it.

Dear Debbie,
   We saw Venus today,
and it's a little smaller
than Earth, but much
more dangerous. It is
covered with thick, poisonous,
acid clouds. The air has
enough heat and pressure to
crack spaceships! Venus
has lots of earsplitting
thunder, and lightning, too.
   Wish you were here!
      Your friend,
      Simon

Debbie DeMilo
201 Flytrap St.
Cupid City, NY
            12420

VENUS

EARTH

MOON

Dear Mom,
   Guess what? We saw the
actual footprints of the first
astronaut to walk on Earth's
moon—Neil Armstrong. We left
our footprints, too.   They'll
last forever because there's
no wind or rain to destroy them.
I guess a meteor might crash
down on them. That's how the
moon's craters were made. I
hope a meteor doesn't land on us!
           Love,
             Tanisha
P.S. On Earth I weigh 72 pounds—
     here I weigh only 12!

Luna Cee
100 Crescent Ave.
Crater Lake, OR
U.S.A. 97604

meteor

OUCH!

Earth

MARS

Dear Uncle Martin,
  Here is a poem about Mars~
RED PLANET
  Canyons,
  Volcanoes,
  Clouds of dust,
  Boulders,
  Craters,
  The color of rust.
Scientists think Mars
used to have water in
rivers or oceans. It still
has ice at the poles, but
it's a desert planet now.
  See you!   Love,
          Lin

P.S. Mars has 2 small moons.

PHOBOS
DEIMOS

Mr. Martin Greenman
#4 Canal Street
Venice, FL
U.S.A.   33595

I am so thirsty!

Look at the thousands of asteroids we're passing. The asteroid belt is between the small, rocky inner planets and the giant outer planets.

ASTEROID

Dear Mom and Dad,
Dr. Quasar says that asteroids are big chunks of rock. Most of them stay in the asteroid belt, but one could drift out of orbit and crash into a planet (even Earth!)

Love,
Simon

P.S. Don't bother wearing helmets- the chance of an asteroid hitting Earth is very small.

Mr. and Mrs. Goldbloom
1000 Collision Road
Bumpers, NJ
U.S.A. 08857

JUPITER is made of gases and liquids that swirl around. It has the GREAT RED SPOT which is really a huge storm.

Dear Stella,
   Did U know that Jupiter is the BIGGEST planet? It has colorful stripes, + a very faint ring system made of dust. 👁 think the weirdest thing is that 🪐 has no solid crust of land. Maybe it is sort of like melted 🍦! C U later... Your bro,
   Ray
P.S. 🪐 has 16 ☾'s.

Stella Corona
93 Shady Lane
Sun Valley, Idaho
U.S.A. 83353

JUPITER

SATURN'S hundreds of rings look solid from a distance, but they are made mostly of many small pieces of ice.

Dear Mom and Dad,
    Here is a poem for you~
SATURN'S RINGS
Snowballs
And icebergs
Drifting in space
Around the planet
The icy chunks race.

I think Saturn is the prettiest planet. It has more than 20 moons (scientists keep finding new ones!) Love, Lin

Mr. and Mrs. Chang
808 Circle Court
Loopdeloop, CA
U.S.A.   90287

SATURN

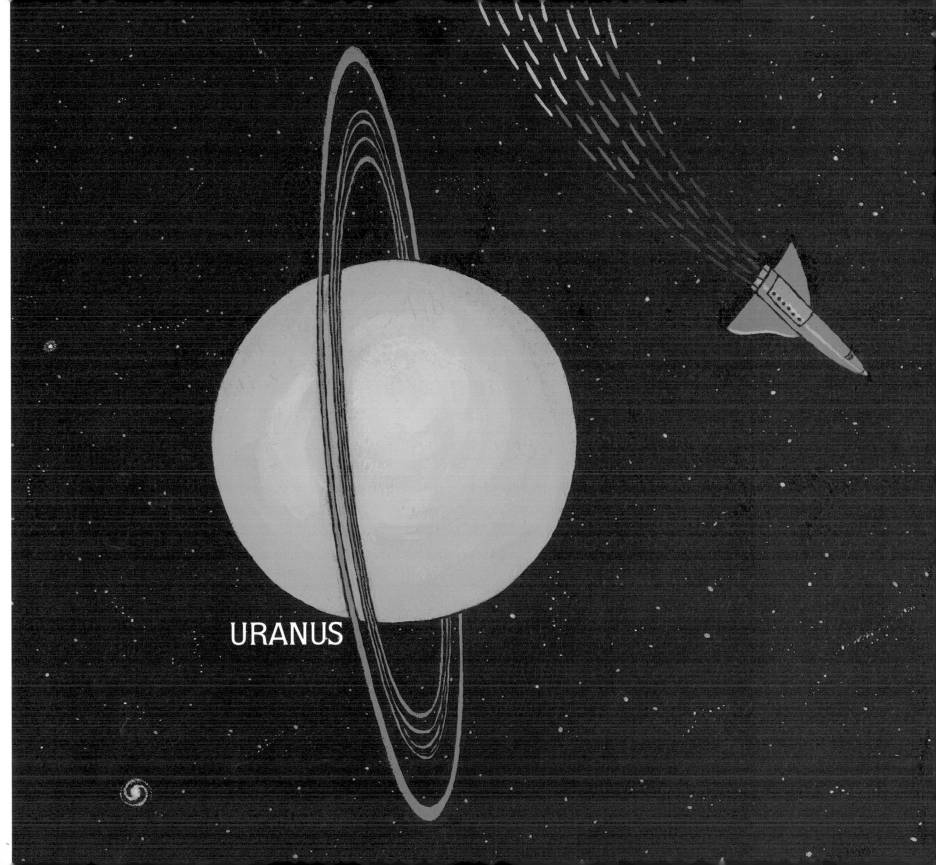

URANUS

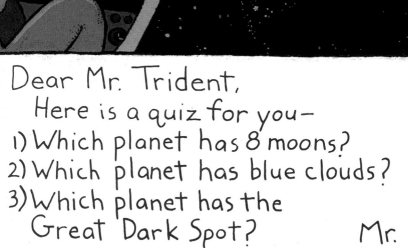

NEPTUNE

Here is PLUTO, the outermost planet.
The Sun looks so tiny from here!
That's why the outer planets are so cold.
Dear Grandfather,
Can you believe it- we are 6 billion kilometers from home! Pluto is the very smallest planet, and the last one in the solar system (as far as we know.) Scientists think another planet could be hiding out here. Maybe when I grow up, I'll discover it!
See you soon- Love,
MINDA
P.S. Pluto has one big moon, called Charon.
PLANET X?
Joe Thunderhawk
248 Final Trail
Tail End, TX
U.S.A. 77050
It's cold out here!

PLUTO

Charon